HOLLYWOOD ALIENS

HOLLYWOOD ALIENS

PARIS TOSEN

Canada

This is a work of nonfiction.

Published by CreateSpace Independent Publishing Platform

This material deals with a subject that has no official recognition and does not exist according to the best scientific minds on the planet.

The author has been recognized as a genuine Stelan, as defined, and is an interstellar and interdimensional cultural expert. His opinions have been expressed.

This book also available as an ebook.

ISBN 978-1511890540

www.tosen.ca
www.stelan.ca

CONTENTS

PROLOGUE
Threats from Space

JACK: Don't fight it, Miles. It's no use. Sooner or later you'll have to go to sleep.

KAUFFMAN: Miles, you and I are scientific men. You can understand the wonder of what's happened. Now just think, less than a month ago, Santa Mira was like any other town, people with nothing but problems—then out of the sky came a solution, seeds drifting through space for years took root in a farmer's field. From the seeds came pods, which had the power to reproduce themselves in the exact likeness of any form of life.

MILES: So that's how it began, out of the sky.

KAUFFMAN: Your new bodies are growing in there. They are taking you over, cell for cell, atom for atom. There's no pain. Suddenly, when you are asleep they'll absorb your minds, your memories, and you're reborn into an untroubled world

MILES: Where everyone's the same?

KAUFFMAN: Exactly.

MILES: *(shaking head in disbelief)* What a world.

Invasion of the Body Snatchers (1956)

Aliens are a threat to the entire human race, according to Hollywood. Outer space is saturated with a grotesque milieu of evil space monsters. The size and shape of the alien is almost always unique, there's no shortage of imagination; but, overall these are all creatures bent on destruction; determined to wipe out the human civilization for the lowest common denominator; expert in serial mass murder and have a creepiness–coupled with sometimes ninja-like camouflage abilities—found in any good story on sociopathic and genocidal behavior. These movie alien characteristics have tainted the global prejudice on the true nature of an interstellar and interdimensional class of people. While the world has indulged in these grotesque fantasies, their real reasons for their creation have remained obscured. My intimate connection to the vast variety of nonhuman races, re-established during the last 10 years, have shown me that the Hollywood version of an alien race is fundamentally flawed, and the flaw is on purpose.

Many alien films are in fact horror films that employ extraterrestrial bodies to splash on the gore in unimaginable and grotesque ways, suggesting in part that human beings are not capable of such horrific behavior, while only a small few comedic pictures portray aliens as bumbling idiots, *Earth Girls Are Easy* (1988), in possession of an advanced interplanetary ship. In almost every story we find government knowledge, and secrecy, of ETs and the interference from clandestine intelligence units, and all kinds of stolen or back-engineered alien technology.

My first contact with interstellar men and women was when I was a young boy in Vancouver, British Columbia. Although those early experiences faded from my memory during my teenage years, and beyond, they did resurface in 2004 and much more profoundly in 2005. Overall, I can say that I have met many kinds of interstellar races, in every situation imaginable, having written and spoken extensively to the fact, and I am convinced that by and large, with some exceptions, these races of people are altruistic, well-meaning and far more technologically advanced than the human race. They have also been here for a very long time and haven't necessarily participated in any of the movie storylines we've been led to believe (and there's no evidence to say otherwise aside from UFO sightings and visitation stories). Moreover, my 2006 public outing as a genuine *Stelan* (a person whose origins are from offplanet), documented in my memoirs and publicly available video materials, gives me intimate and exclusive access to a set of ethnic qualities that have never been available to us.

  The evolution and continuation of pre-packaged alien themes as a form of entertainment demands a book, even if in a shorter format, that objectively and adequately represents the people who have been woefully under-represented, the extraterrestrials. While the past seven decades have seen hundreds of possible alien cultures, stamping their necessity into our entertainment industry, any scholarly alien study is largely absent. The classified nature of this topic, and the suppressed and censored discussions, has been the key reason why this field has remained one-sided and heavily biased. There have been many books and documentaries on the subject of UFOs and ETs, *Abduction: Human Encounters with Aliens* (Dr. John E. Mack), *The Day After Roswell* (Philip J. Corso) or *Awakening* (Mary Rodwell, RN), but we haven't seen any ethnic studies in alien cultures. Furthermore, the misrepresentation of advanced extraterrestrial races of people has led to a distorted and discriminatory view of all offplanet life forms.

This book attempts to bridge some of those cultural prejudices and it distinguishes itself from other extraterrestrial studies by accepting the presence of nonhumans as being true; and it insists that these starry people are first and foremost "people," a stark contrast to the evil monsters found in films. It is a concise book and an important introduction to broader interstellar discussions.

There are no accidents in Hollywood. Filmmakers spend a great deal of time conceiving then writing a screenplay. Having written a number of screenplays myself, I can attest to the fact that screenwriting is an art that takes a lot of practice, kind of like painting, and not all scripts are worthy of production. Film production is a subjective business entirely wrapped around the obsession to tell the audience a great story, and hopefully to make money at doing so. It's gambling with other people's money. Most films never make money. Independent films tend to tell real stories about real people. An Indie film is lucky to find a distributor who will market it to 100 art house theatres. This is mostly because film producers know that audiences don't want real stories about real people. What do audiences want? Audiences want to be entertained; hence the advent of the science fiction genre.

I hope to highlight a consistent horror characteristic with any extraterrestrial experience, with films frequently using terror as a device to drive a plot forward. Inevitably, America is the dominant producer of alien-themed science fiction films, and probably all of the films produced since 1950 have come out of Hollywood to one degree or another. This book focuses on the most widely released alien films starting in 1950 up until 2012, with the exclusion of comic book film adaptations (making the exception for the 2012 box-office smash *The Avengers* for its alien invasion aspect and *Guardians of the Galaxy*).

A film with an alien theme, for the purposes of discussion in this book, is any film that contains a significant extraterrestrial or offplanet character, even if not necessarily the antagonist or protagonist. Oftentimes, the alien element is contained in a background story of a character and sometimes an offplanet theme is derived because of an inter-dimensional element or has something to do with the false nature of reality, as in the cult film *The Matrix* (1999). Alien-themed science fiction is often dressed in psychopathic creatures from space as a means to psychologically terrorize an audience and to highlight the moral integrity of a unified human resistance, for example the movie *Independence Day* (1997) and its US-led globalized resistance.

The adoption of a repulsive alien antagonist (a grotesque and evil creature), a necessary film device to drive the story forward, is at the same time linked to the protection of a homogenous human civilization from any extraterrestrial contact, verily the cinematic pastiches discourage any interstellar hope, aside from a comic book hero like *Superman*, a lone spark of hope who is admittedly an alien. These pervasive fear-based scenarios and cultural divisions, by presenting anything from space as evil or having evil intention or a dark agenda, have managed to distort the view and opinions of society regarding extraterrestrial reconciliation.

It can be argued that the alien invasion genre maximized the box office potential and provided a reliable avenue for a least a mediocre profit. And this is indeed the case, as we'll see later on in the book, since the alien invasion storyline, at least among the Top 100 films in North America, brought in $6 billion in revenue compared to only $1.1 billion in alien films *without* an alien invasion. This is gleaned from *Box Office Mojo*.

The "threat from space formula," shared by 90% of all alien films, constitutes a threat from the unknown, suggesting that human beings perceive the unknown with unprecedented fear and rejection and that the filmmakers are merely capitalizing on those anxieties. But is the unknown always a threat? The question is almost answered in the positive. Even a film like *Starman* (1984), which earned Jeff Bridges an Academy Award nomination for Best Actor, the strange visitor to the planet, invited to visit in peace finds humanity savage and is hunted by a cold-blooded NSA agent.

Audiences come to these films, not for their horror aspects, which is often argued the case, rather they want to see what's in space but that they don't want to like it. It is as if they want to reject it, to be grossed out by it so as to justify their own inability to handle the unknown. In a psychological paradox, human beings have been conditioned to explore the unknown but to be repulsed by it; therefore, they go home reminded that their life is perfect as it is. Why change anything?

The repulsiveness of the unknown, we often forget, is intimately linked to clandestine military operations which are well-aware of actual extraterrestrials, even owning back-engineered machines and devices and scientific theories such as time travel. And it has been demonstrated in recent films like *Argo* (2012), a dramatization of a declassified operation headed by CIA operative Tony Mendez, or *Confessions of a Dangerous Mind* (2002), a biographical spy film about a popular game show producer who was also a high-level CIA assassin, that the CIA has agents in the film and TV production. Although you may never have heard of Phil Strub, the entertainment liaison since 1989 at the Department of Defense, he's the decision maker who approves scripts before any military hardware or personnel are rented out; and the military doesn't like a negative depiction of their organization, especially not when fighting alien invaders. In exchange for basically free hardware and military personnel, film producers willingly modify their screen stories to the Pentagon's recommendations. The Pentagon doesn't believe in extraterrestrials and supports the alien invasion scenario wholeheartedly if for only the fact that it provides ample ground for military training and propaganda.

The salient link between Hollywood and National Security goes back to July 26, 1947, the day that President Harry Truman signed the National Security Act, which eventually led to the formation of the CIA, NSA, NSC, the Pentagon, and the Secretary of Defense. The complete restructuring of American security happened, by chance, to take place just 18 days after the famous incident at Roswell, New Mexico whereby a flying saucer was shot down and crashed.

Roswell and US National Security didn't happen at the same time by accident unless they both used the same planners. No, the restructuring of homeland defense was necessary to prevent another Roswell, the 9/11 event of the late-40s. Governments don't act impulsively because they have voters and there's a thing called Congress that needs to approve important decisions. For every new bill pushed forward there is equally any number of politicians pushing backward. The National Security Act saw no real resistance because it was hinged on the threat of an interstellar disclosure. Three years later is when we saw the first of many alien-themed films. Coincidence? You be the judge. I don't believe in coincidence. I will take the position that organizations like the CIA and NSA have a vested interest in making sure that society is perennially afraid of all extraterrestrial life forms, even to say that society remains repulsed by anything in outer space. We are a people who do not like space.

It doesn't take much to realize that alien disinformation is so widespread that films that make very little cinematic sense, *Battleship* (2012) and *Battle: LA* (2011) are overt forms of public brainwashing designed from the start to distance the human being from the nonhuman being. It is often the case, for example *The Thing* (1982) and *Signs* (2002) that the alien monster central to the story is by default evil and menacing and the main characters have no interest to understand its motivations unless it will help them survive.

Audiences also enjoy alien films because as menacing and murderous as the aliens are they are also extremely advanced and present humanity with new levels of understanding. These space creatures appear to activate an inner desire to see the technologies of the future, for example motherships and artificial intelligence, but the horror of the process makes people afraid of the future. It is like allowing a person to eat a spoonful of chocolate cheesecake and then to be shown a photograph of an obese and ugly self-portrait, which at its core is found in mind control manuals. The alien is advanced and in possession of new forms of energy, but, at the exact same time, the alien is a threat that must be completely destroyed.

There is never any real attempt to sequester the antimatter propulsion drives because it almost always comes down to the fact that the entire mothership must be vaporized, and so any of the possible benefits of an encounter are completely taken away. This is often what happened under experiments with Ivan Pavlov, a scientist who used various stimuli to condition a specific reflex from a dog, for example ringing a bell to make the dog salivate. When it came to aliens, filmmakers were conditioning audiences to fear the benefits of advanced civilizations. And in cases where the alien's technology could not be destroyed, such as the film *The Thing*, the setting is so remote (the frozen wastes of the Antarctic) and the survivors so decimated that there's no chance of ever returning to the locale.

In *Planet of the Apes* (1968), originally written by Rod Serling and drafted from the 1963 French novel *La Planète des Singes* by Pierre Boulle, the protagonist is unable to warn the world because he is in the wrong time dilation. *Forbidden Planet* (1956) was famous for being the first to depict a man-made starship and the explorations of another planet, but, the technologies of that planet had to be left behind in order to escape alive and therefore provided no benefit to human science. This is the general theme of science fiction pieces. There is an advanced technology but there is a monster and to destroy the monster means the destruction or abandonment of the technology. It's a zero-sum game.

In recent years there has been an increased overlapping with the science fiction and military war genres in such a manner that incites and involves unparalleled interplanetary war. *Star Wars, Star Trek*, and the *Transformers* franchise are all large-scale epics with unprecedented military themes. The days of *The Man Who Fell to Earth* (1976) and the family-friendly, and one of my favorites as a kid, *Escape to Witch Mountain* (1975) are long gone. The Pentagon has now staked its claim in UFO studies and we can infer that the Pentagon is also well aware of the presence of interstellar cultures on this planet and wants to ensure that no amount of reconciliation ever takes place.

CHAPTER 1
An Alien Film Retrospective

In order to come to a new understanding, I decided to study the most reliable data on aliens, Hollywood science fiction movies. Starting in the 1950s and ending in the most recent year of 2012, I catalogued alien-themed feature films distributed in the North American market. Analyses of the alien catalogue of feature films revealed propaganda that helps explain why the public has never been given a full UFO disclosure, and why governments had decided to maintain a UFO cover-up, and denied any extraterrestrial presence as having any validity.

Breakdown
Total Films Overall, 1950-2012: **10,000** (approx.)
Total Alien Films, 1950-2012: **250** (2.5%)
Total Evil Alien Films, 1950-2012: **228** (91%)
Total Propaganda-free Alien Films, 1950-2012: **22** (9%)

By concentrating on available evidence found in stylized, expensive, and egregious alien-themed films (and franchises), and using my own improvised methodologies, I have put together some basic statistics on extraterrestrials when represented as entertainment and it explains why the fear of offplanet visitors is so pervasive. I have examined 250 movies with alien-themes or story lines, previously released from 1950 to 2012 in North America, for the presence of evil-minded aliens (vs altruistic aliens, which we discuss in the third article), the kind of monster required to spin a science fiction yarn worth a bag of overly-priced popcorn.

Average alien films/year: 4
Total Alien Films (1950-1959): 30
Total Alien Films (1960-1969): 16
Total Alien Films (1970-1979): 27
Total Alien Films (1980-1989): 57
Total Alien Films (1990-1999): 53
Total Alien Films (2000-2009): 49
Total Alien Films (2010): 2
Total Alien Films (2011): 10
Total Alien Films (2012): 6

The evidence was previously understood to be presented in a benign and theatrical manner. Alien monsters and invasions were passed off as entertainment and used to justify military basterds. But the decontamination of the evidence that removed the illusory storyline and diminished the relevance of the celebrities which can conceal the clandestine themes, I discovered evil aliens 73% of the time. After more than 63 years of data, I found that 3 out of every 4 movies have evil aliens with plans to destroy the world or mankind, usually for reasons that don't make any sense (eg for our water). Most of the remaining films contain a mix of story elements, good vs evil, and almost always included military-style skirmishes, including the handful of alien-themed comedies.

A good example of a hybrid story was the film *Star Trek II: The Wrath of Khan* (1983) because it contained both kinds of alien characters, evil (Khan) and good (Kirk). *The Empire Strikes Back* (1980), another one of my selections, also had both thematic elements, Darth Vader vs Luke Skywalker, and because of this was not considered to be a pure "evil alien film." So the 73-percent figure is exclusively evil. I do include these other films later on in the discussion in order to provide a more comprehensive distribution of derogatory science fiction films. The highest percentage of alien-themed films were produced between 1970 and 1989 with the two domestic box-office standouts including *Star Wars* ($461 million) and *E.T.: the Extra-Terrestrial* ($435 million). Nearly all of the alien films in the 20 years prior to 1970 portrayed aliens as pure monsters.

In the alien genre there are eight basic types of aliens, all of which go about their antagonistic duties albeit under different circumstances. The first type, **Alien Serial Killer**, is unique because it is almost irrelevant that the creature hails from outer space. What its interstellar origins provides is a multitude of advanced ways in which to eviscerate the helpless human astronauts, for example, the 8-foot xenomorph with acid blood in the *Alien* franchise or the shape-shifter in *The Thing*. *Predator* was about aliens who came to earth to hunt humans and to skin them alive

The **Alien Veggie Monster** is another cool kind of creature. Filmmakers, probably against vegetarianism, created monsters out of plants. This is where we find the plantlike pods of *The Invasion of the Body Snatchers* or the walking plants in the 1951 picture *Day of the Triffids*.

There are many films that have used the **Evil Alien Invader** model to destroy the world. The evil alien comes in many shapes and sizes but its aim is to take over the planet, to wipe out humanity, or to simply destroy the world. The alien robots, Decepticons, wanted to take over the earth and to convert it to a machine world in *The Transformers*. The 2008 remake of *The Day the Earth Stood Still* starring Keanu Reeves demonstrated why an alien would wipe all of humanity in order to protect the planet from imminent ecocide. *Independence Day* was an explicit invasion scenario starting from the first image of a giant mothership. *Signs* was an invasion story as was the blockbuster film, *The Avengers*. Tim Burton's version of *Mars Attacks!* was about an all-out invasion from little Martians with ray guns.

A rarer type of film is the **Intergalactic Ambassador** whereby an offworld being, or group, comes to the planet for peaceful purposes only to surprisingly discover just how savage humanity still is. The best modern attempts were probably Spielberg's *Close Encounters of the Third Kind* and *E.T.: the Extra-Terrestrial.* But *Starman* also fairly represented how an alien ambassador would be unwelcome on Earth. The 1951 classic piece *The Day the Earth Stood Still* remains as the best overall example of an intergalactic ambassador.

We also find alien monsters that defy shapes and sizes, **Space Entities**, and are therefore referred to in mysterious ways, even to their nebulous forms like *The Blob* (1958), an amoeba-like alien that grows as it eats humans. There is also the *The Hidden* (1987) about a slug-like alien that can enter a body through the mouth and take over the human. And in *Lifeforce* (1985) we find three space vampires that suck the life force out of their victims in order to stay alive. The Russian film *Solaris* depicted a giant alien ocean that was capable of reading your thoughts and manifesting them.

The **Interstellar Bacteria** angle has also been explored in *The Andromeda Strain* and *The Invasion*. And the **Stranded Alien** theme has been used in many films, notably in *Starman*, the last of his kind, trapped on the earth with only hours left before he dies, and *The Man Who Fell to Earth*, about a humanoid alien who crashes on the planet and becomes stranded. He later becomes rich but also an alcoholic. The robot aliens in *Transformers* are also trapped on earth after their home planet had been destroyed.

Finally we can add the **Interdimensional Villain** type. One of the best examples is Agent Smith from *The Matrix*. He is basically a computer program and that is because reality is a large computer simulation. We find others, even if not always villains, in *The Adjustment Bureau*. In *The Adventures of Buckaroo Banzai Across the 8th Dimension* we get to see what interdimensional agents look like, both good and bad. And even in the cult film *They Live*, directed by John Carpenter, we find that the capitalistic world we so love is actually the creation of a group of multidimensional colonialists who have co-opted humanity's ego and enslaved the world.

I did not fully take into account the box office or cultural impact of any of these films, only to a smaller degree, perhaps something to consider as part of a larger discussion. But it would be so subjective that it might be hard to accurately analyze the data. Did *The Invasion of the Body Snatchers* torment society more than *Escape to Witch Mountain* inspired and entertained audiences? Director Ridley Scott's science fiction horror classic *Alien* ($105 million) in 1979 was a cultural landmark, spawning a number of similarly scary sequels, all of which have nothing to do with actual extraterrestrial races, but that did not diminish any ticket sales. The film borrowed heavily from the 1951 interstellar horror film dating back to *The Thing From Another World* ($2 million), also preserved in the National Film Registry, and its two remakes as *The Thing* in 1982 ($20 million) and 2011 ($27 million). The James Cameron sequel *Aliens* used the tag line: "This Time It's War."

Contrast the *Alien* media franchise, with three sequels and three prequels (so far), with the stand-alone science fiction-drama *Close Encounters of the*

Third Kind and you can see how Steven Spielberg's tale of scientists, government researchers, and UN experts investigating heightened UFO activities in the US eventually centered in Wyoming and the arrival of a giant mothership did not have the same cultural impact around the world.

Ironically, Spielberg not only borrows from former astrophysicist and UFOlogist J. Allen Hynek but he depicts the US Army deceiving the public while setting up a secret landing site for extraterrestrials. A horror sequel was never produced.

Do the 6 *Alien* films and the 3 films of *The Thing* balance out with *Close Encounters* and *E.T.*? Nine films against two. Is *Star Wars* an accurate representation of interstellar cultures? Do all offplanet races have laser rifles and are fighting against imperial armies? Or are there more benevolent races that do not carry weapons and instead prefer a domestic lifestyle. Can aliens cook without a lightsaber? Do they use hospitals and doctors to treat the wounded or are aliens designed from the get-go to be like pork for the meat grinder?

Avatar in 2009, a box-office giant with $2.8 billion in worldwide ticket sales, pioneered a different kind of alien race reminiscent of American Indian culture stationed on another planet that fought against human invaders. But James Cameron has the political heft to get away with holistic ETs. He's in the process of filming three Avatar sequels to be release in 2016, 2017, and 2018. Not many filmmakers can do this. One of the standout alien films in the eighties was John Carpenter's *Starman*, about an alien response to an invitation from a space probe. The ETs send a scout ship which is shot down by the US government and the surviving starman, superbly played by Jeff Bridges, coerces a woman to aid his rendezvous with his mothership. It earned $28 million at the domestic box office.

Even we have a library of 250 theatrical releases based on human concepts of alien races, we still do not know much about alien cultures. During the entire 1960s we saw 16 alien film releases, the fewest out of all decades sampled. The year 2011 alone released 10 alien films. Did our preoccupation with NASA and the moon landings reduce our fear of outer space? Why was it in the 1980s that 57 alien films were made? Was that because the Apollo Space Program had ended too abruptly? Project Apollo put 12 astronauts on the moon at a cost of $25 billion. That's about $2 billion for each astronaut.

At today's prices, it would cost $13 billion for each astronaut. Apollo closed down in 1975. These films followed: *The Man Who Fell to Earth, Close*

Encounters of the Third Kind, Star Wars, The Black Hole, Star Trek: The Motion Picture.

CHAPTER 2
The False Alien Threat

"There is abundant evidence that we are being contacted, that civilizations have been visiting us for a very long time, that their appearance is bizarre from any kind of traditional materialistic western point of view, that these visitors use the technologies of consciousness, they use toroids, they use co-rotating magnetic discs for their propulsion systems, that seems to be the common denominator of the UFO phenomenon and how they can work, manipulate time and space locally so that they can have their own anti-gravity propulsion and their own field of energy."

DR. BRIAN O'LEARY, former NASA
Astronaut and Physics Professor

Hollywood's obsession with alien horror and alien wars should not be taken lightly, especially when you understand the real motives and altruistic characteristics of interstellar cultures. My initial results highlight another very important fact: if 73% of all alien-themed films in the past six decades portray aliens bent on destroying the world, and no credible alien invasion has ever presented itself in the last 12,000 years of human history (because there would be documentation to prove otherwise), then this evidence supports the notion that there is a unified message being broadcast to society. The message is that "aliens are a threat to humankind."

Thank you for signing the petition asking the Obama Administration to acknowledge an extraterrestrial presence here on Earth.

The U.S. government has no evidence that any life exists outside our planet, or that an extraterrestrial presence has contacted or engaged any member of the human race. In addition, there is no credible information to suggest that any evidence is being hidden from the public's eye.

Phil Larson, White House Office of Science & Technology Policy, November 8, 2011

My results bring to question the long-held position of governments, military organizations, and space agencies—that no extraterrestrial presence has ever contacted the human race and that no evidence is being hidden from the public. Why? Because if no extraterrestrial presence had ever contacted the human race then by definition we would never be able to know the true disposition of an offplanet race. There would be no evidence to do so.

Given the fact that the greater majority of alien films contain evil alien monsters, and this theme is consistently funded and supported by the Pentagon, whose Hollywood division allocates the hardware (jets, aircraft carriers, tanks, Humvees) and military training (shooting assault rifles and wearing cargo pants), it would make sense that the producers or filmmakers have an agenda, and that they've been informed that aliens are a threat to humankind, the general position; for if the truth was unknown and no extraterrestrials had ever been present then there would be far less evil alien invasion films than there are today.

We cannot excuse all alien invasion films as happening by accident or without any prior inspiration, and we know that good filmmakers and smart producers will have done their research prior to starting any feature film. Large studios have many executives and researchers who are paid to do their market research in order to protect their investments in creative properties. A film usually takes five or more years to reach pre-production and scripts are highly scrutinized and rewritten in order to have the best screenplay possible.

None of this is strange to those who are aware of interstellar cultures and the clandestine agencies which are determined to ruin any form of genuine reconciliation with star people. And there are millions of experiencers and witnesses and UFO researchers who make every government position look flaccid, unpresidential, and deceptive. What we have in Hollywood is either intent without motive or intent with a secret motive.

We have big budget science fiction movies being funded from thin air and every filmmaker or wannabe producer knows how difficult it is to raise money for even the best script on earth, so how is it that producers can get money for extraterrestrial pornography films like *Battle: LA* and *Battleship*, or even *War of the Worlds*?

Universal Pictures invested $220 million in *Battleship* (2012) and hired Peter Berg to direct a film that had nothing to do with the classic board game, though that was their excuse, and everything to do with a large-scale unwarranted and completely senseless alien invasion peppered with pretty girls the likes of Rihanna, a pop star, and Brooklyn Decker, a fashion model. Besides flopping at the box office, *Battleship* highlighted a clandestine motivation behind the continued discriminatory practices in the science fiction film business when it came to extraterrestrials for only an agenda could convince intelligent investors to hand over a quarter of a billion dollars to a bunch of filmmakers.

One of the ways in which a unified message takes shape is if there is a unified motivation. Some group or agency with government and military connections, and with an intimate access to Hollywood producers and filmmakers, wants the public to believe that any extraterrestrial presence is a sign of doom and they have done a good job so far at spreading this disinformation and setting up storylines the likes of which make Santa Claus look like Jesus and the Easter Bunny as your long-lost cousin.

It's been over 60 years of evil alien propaganda and I think it's time that we stop watching these social reengineering programs and instead demand that extraterrestrials receive a more balanced representation in films. Not all aliens have a UFO.

Unless an educated and informed producer is behind an alien-themed film, negative propaganda should be expected as well as a clandestine agenda that implicates some level of the government, unless there is some evidence to explain otherwise.

CHAPTER 3
Evidence of a Secret Agenda

The box office battle with alien-themed films has really been about evil aliens, bent on the destruction of others, versus altruistic aliens, concerned for the welfare of others. The worst of the worst in evil alien propaganda total 182 films, but when the hybrid pictures are included, they contain a mixture of good and evil elements and are mostly centered on warlike situations, that total jumps to 227 films, or about 91%. The remaining 22 films, 9% of the total, can be considered to portray aliens with altruistic characteristics. We could split that figure as well to isolate accurate portrayals (4%) versus aliens with ambiguous characteristics (5%).

Here is a sample of the kinds of films I have determined to be in the 9% group: *Cocoon, Contact, Knowing, The Man Who Fell to Earth, Starman, Close Encounters of the Third Kind, The Day the Earth Stood Still* (1951), and

Hangar 18. I would consider these films to be generally free of disinformation and definitely more sided with extraterrestrial characteristics.

Probably 100% of these altruistic alien features contain strong depictions of government interference, usually in the likes of agents from the National Security Agency and many of them have military engagements. I have also included pseudo-extraterrestrials in my examination of these films from films like *The Adjustment Bureau* and *K-PAX*. While *The Matrix* didn't make the altruistic cut it was included in the discussion and this is because of the synthetic nature of reality.

In fact, we could say that the *Star Wars* subculture was educated on old ideas of spacefaring people and that the *Matrix* subculture more accurately reflects the technological space that many extraterrestrials inhabit, and also why more and more people think of ETs as interdimensional people. This represents an evolutionary leap that happened between the mid-1970s and the late-1990s and reveals some (likely) DNA adjustments during that period. When we step back and examine the 1950s alien subculture we find almost no friendly variants and are faced with example after example of monsters from outer space.

From 1950 to 1969 about 95% of all alien-themed films portrayed extraterrestrials as evil. That depiction started to shift in the seventies starting in the 1975 release of *Escape to Witch Mountain* where the aliens were a cute boy and girl who were escaping evil government agents. Its domestic take was only $20 million. That figure pales in comparison to the $461 million that *Star Wars* generated with its dark empire and interstellar battles. Even the horror piece *Alien* generated $80 million domestically, four times as much. Twenty years later, Roland Emmerich's *Independence Day*, about an all-out alien invasion without any motive whatsoever, earned $306 million despite its 150-minute runtime. It earned a further $511 million overseas. Whatever positive effects were generated from *Escape* has long been wiped out.

Over the last 63 years, ending in 2012, the top evil alien films in the Top 100 box office generated a whopping $6 billion in domestic sales (83%) while altruistic alien films only brought in $1.2 billion (17%), and that is because I included *Avatar* and its nearly $800 million haul alongside *E.T.*; otherwise the numbers would be far worse. *Avatar* isn't the ideal altruistic choice but the alien Na'vi culture was so remarkably scripted and drawn out that the military skirmishes are almost a secondary or tertiary plot device. In any case we have six times more evil alien propaganda than extraterrestrial truth and balanced opinions to deal with. Put another way, if there was a secret agenda, which I think we've established that there is given the emphasis on evil alien invasion story lines and dark agendas, then their best films had six times the domestic reach, not to mention the influence on a worldwide audience. Not only are 91% of Hollywood alien films evil-themed, but of the 20 alien-themed films in the Top 100 movies, 18 of them (90%) portray aliens as evil.

The public relations battle is being lost. The altruistic message is overshadowed by the dark empire of alien invasion movies and as long as these propaganda juggernauts persist there is no chance at any interstellar reconciliation. Again, it isn't an accident that *War of the Worlds* gets remade twice and *Starman* is a stand-alone film. It isn't an accident that the *Alien* franchise has six films and *Close Encounters of the Third Kind* is a one-of-a-kind. When they remade *The Day the Earth Stood Still* in 2008 they completely ignored the genuine and intelligent qualities of the 1951 original. In the remake, the alien has decided that humanity is a threat to the planet and must be exterminated in order for the planet's ecology to survive.

In the way that we are fed disinformation in the evil alien franchises we are similarly educated with the altruistic pieces and are able to hear the thoughts and ideas of our genetic parents. A good example of this is the film *Hangar 18*. Released in 1980 it was a typical Roswell-type story but the script is lined with sentences taken out of some book on Ufology. Sometimes even science fiction-horror films contain elements of truth mixed in with the deception. Consider the

1978 remake of *Invasion of the Body Snatchers* and its concern that people were being duplicated and replaced by their clones. This could have been an interpretation of a real life situation.

When the leadership fails to lead and the schools fail to teach, films can provide those essential courses and these altruistic films have at least brought some peace of mind to members of the population who have been visited, or tormented, and want to keep it private. But the disparity between genuine aliens on film and their evil counterparts is discouraging, and 90% of the box office kings are full of disinformation.

This ratio 90:10 is what is preventing our reconciliation with interstellar cultures and I think this research only highlights one of the principle causes of anti-ET thinking. If Senator A had 10% of the votes and Senator B had 90% of the votes which Senator do you think will win an election? Senator B. And they will justify the win because of the high percentage of voter turnout. But when the system is corrupt and the voters have been brainwashed to believe in lies and have been told that any extraterrestrial contact will lead to the destruction of the planet then society will always vote for Senator B. And Senator B is a UFO Cover-Up because Senator A is a UFO Disclosure.

Until the public realizes that they have not only been brainwashed for 63 years to believe in alien misinformation, but that this protocol is still in force, until the public is aware of that then they will likely continue to vote for a UFO Cover-Up (Senator B) because they are still afraid of monsters from outer space. Now if they realize the deceptive tactics purposely employed against them and they realize that they have been misinformed and that not all aliens will eat their children and that no alien invasion has ever taken place then and only then will they possibly consider voting for Senator A, a full and proper UFO Disclosure. And I think at this point it's time to vote for some fresh thinking on the subject. At the very least, since a disclosure may not be immediately achievable, be aware that there are agencies who are actively distorting the

truth of this sensitive situation and their
interests do not only include films.

CHAPTER 4
Extraterrestrial Capitalists

The impact of extraterrestrial culture on
Hollywood was an extremely new phenomenon,
but, historically speaking, there was plenty of
real-world evidence of extraterrestrial contact—
Egyptian pyramids, crop circles, abductions,
UFOs and flying saucer sightings, and then
Roswell, culminating in an entirely new National
Security Act for the United States signed in the
same month and year as the crashed disc in New
Mexico. As a result of the militarized
information blockade and the censorship of
classified data, the extraterrestrial story spilled
over into the next best thing next to reality,
visual storytelling (aka movies). The fear and
misunderstanding of advanced interplanetary
cultures coupled with fantastic displays of
science and observations of onboard computer
systems yet-to-be-invented resulted in an
entirely new culture, Martians, and their
mysterious red planet.

It started in *Flight to Mars* (1950) and *Invader from Mars* (1953), but soon branched out into outer space in general. The popularity of Martian invaders took a historical leap after the release of the film version of *The War of the Worlds* (1953). This was in addition to the infamous radio drama in 1938 headed by Orson Wells, later earning high regards for making *Citizen Kane* (1941), one of the all-time greatest films, which caused widespread panic in America, and to the original 1898 book version by H.G. Wells. The success of the alien-themed epic would spark the imagination of many young filmmakers for years to come.

It can be argued that the alien invasion storyline was established in 1938 but solidified in 1953 as a formula for almost a guarantee in box office receipts. The "alien invasion" soon enough became the preferred storyline for any films involving aliens, extraterrestrials, or space monsters. Whether human-looking, monstrous entities with acid blood, vegetable pods or intergalactic bacteria, all of them were uniquely coherent in their disgust for human existence.

On the surface the alien-themed science fiction film was sold as entertainment and it didn't take long for society to completely forget that these stories had roots in the real world, but information on extraterrestrials was impossible to come by except from a fragmented, but resilient, UFO community. Through information leaks, disinformation campaigns and from UFO sightings and visitations the film industry had a small but steady trickle of extraterrestrial ideas, which started to break out of its censored and suppressed status as audiences took to *Alien* (1979*), Invasion of the Body Snatchers* (1978), *Close Encounters of the Third Kind* (1977) and *Star Wars* (1977).

The alien monsters from space from the fifties and sixties were replaced by the human-looking intergalactic heroes and villains of the seventies. All of a sudden, filmmakers realized, with a little help from auteurs George Lucas and Steven Spielberg, that there was big money in alien stories. And with the release of *The Empire Strikes Back* (1982) the alien franchise was born. Alien cinema, while appearing as entertainment on the surface, also comes loaded with details and information straight out of the UFO Community and disinformation agents. In the film *Hangar 18* (1980), the protagonist, played by America actor Darren McGavin, discusses his revelation with a team of experts:

MAN #1 (McGavin's character): This is a translation of a document found aboard the spacecraft. Now the translation is very rough and it's incomplete. But what if we can read is true—and there's no reason to doubt that it isn't, then all of the previous information we've had about the origin of mankind and the human race is absolutely false.

MAN #2: What are you talking about, Harry?

MAN #1: This is a report of a previous visitor spacecraft to earth. This report speaks of the capture, training, and the use of certain animals as slaves—both male and female—the slaves worshiped them as gods.

MAN #2: Then what they referred to as animals... were pre-humans?

MAN #1: Yes. The report also speaks to the fact that the female slaves found it a great honor to be chosen to live with and to bear the offspring of the gods.

WOMAN: Good Lord...

MAN #1: You see, it's no coincidence that the spacemen are almost identical to us. It is not, Sarah, a case of two species developing, evolving independently of each other. Those ancient spacemen altered forever our evolution. They are the missing link.

MAN #3: *(standing up)* Do you know what you're saying?

MAN #1: Yes! We, mankind— the human race—are their children.

Hangar 18 (1980)

The film is based on a hypothesis of Eric Van Däniken, the controversial author of *Chariots of the Gods?* (1968), he said that ancient astronauts (extraterrestrials) influenced our ancestors, and the crash in Roswell, New Mexico. Contrast their benevolent message with one from *Invasion of the Body Snatchers* (1978 remake), a story about intergalactic seeds arriving on the planet and duplicating people via plantlike pods. Once duplicated, always during sleep, the original turns to dust. Based on the 1955 science fiction novel, *The Body Snatchers*, written by Jack Finney and directed by Philip Kaufman who later directed *The Right Stuff* (1983), earning four Academy Awards. In the second of four remakes, the terrified victims desperately attempt to wake people up before the entire town is taken over by emotionless drones. But because a pod clone looks exactly like the original in appearance they do not know who to trust. Eventually they try to convince their famous psychiatrist friend (not realizing he was a pod clone) that what they've seen is true:

MATTHEW: "No, David, what you're doing... you're looking at it as if it was human. It was not human.

PSYCHIATRIST (DAVID): Matthew, what else would it be?

MATTHEW: It was something but it was not human.

JACK: It had white hair on it.

MATTHEW: It was growing. I mean the one at Jack's place was... it was like Jack but it wasn't as developed as the one at Elizabeth's place.

JACK: It had tendrils on it.

MATTHEW: The one at Elizabeth's place was duplicating her.

ELIZABETH: *(falling apart emotionally)* And if Matthew hadn't taken me out of there the same thing that's happened to Jeffrey would've happened to me.

PSYCHIATRIST: Elizabeth, would you please tell me in your opinion exactly what is happening?

ELIZABETH: *(in tears)* People are being
duplicated and once it's happened to you
you're part of this thing. It almost happened to
me!

Invasion of the Body Snatchers (1978)

In North America the majority of alien movies
portray the extraterrestrial life form as
inherently evil. These extraterrestrials are
vengeful and repulsive monsters whose mortal
enemy is every member of the human race. It
isn't always explained what caused this
animosity to occur and neither do audiences
care. In *Battle: LA* a supposed expert suggests
that the aliens are invading because of the
precious water. It's about one line off a television
feed, as an off-handed remark. It's unimportant.
The entire picture is military warfare.

  Audiences have been conditioned, over many
decades, to view any offplanet race as a threat to
humanity. On the surface it appears accidental
and irrelevant, to see such a consistent dark
theme in traditional alien cinema such as
Independence Day and *Prometheus* (2012), a
quasi-prequel to *Alien* (1979), but given the
intimate link between film producers and the

UFO industry none of this should be seen as accidental. The likelihood that the Pentagon, a major source for expensive military hardware and expert soldiers, participated in *Battle: LA* and *The War of the Worlds* (2005) without any interest in extraterrestrial matters is extremely slim.

The fixation on monstrous creatures, planetary-grade threats and extinction scenarios of alien cinema is accessible to anyone who has watched a Hollywood science fiction film with an alien theme and requires very little theoretical prognostication or intellectual analysis. Those fixations, because they arose at a time of extraterrestrial secrecy and directly followed the establishment of an entirely new national security apparatus, cannot just be considered as purely entertainment devices.

The Ridley Scott favorite *Alien*, which was inducted into the National Film Registry of the Library of Congress (2002), presents a captivating story of a serial killer in space. And if its six other prequels and sequels are anything to go by, this successful film franchise essentially transports a psychotic human attribute to a distant planetoid and replaces the aggressive human stalker with an extraterrestrial one. These films have nothing to do with any benevolent form of contact with extraterrestrial intelligences, something often handled by not-for-profit organizations such as SETI (Search for Extraterrestrial Intelligence), and instead highlight offworld life forms that pose a threat to human beings.

The militarization of extraterrestrial contact in alien cinema, as found in *Predator* (1987) and Super 8 (2011), goes back to the period of early suppression of extraterrestrial knowledge. These films, and others, highlight the involvement of the military and government agencies (eg CIA, NSA, NSC) in a fictional subject that has no official reference. With only small shifts in film scope and aesthetics, the stranded alien films such as the comedy *Paul* (2011) and the drama *Starman* at the same time contain government and military interference, and rather than dismissing these elements as insignificant they have to be understood within the context of a widespread UFO Cover-Up. Even threats from interstellar bacteria, *The Andromeda Strain* (1971), or self-replicating microorganisms, *The Invasion of the Body Snatchers* (original 1956, remakes, 1978, 1993 and 2007), equally rely on police and National Guard as a means of population containment and control.

 The microbial extraterrestrial invader, now a sub-genre found in Hollywood, is also an acceptable deadly threat to the human race. Admittedly, the alien-themed science fiction film doesn't equal the traditional film genres, but it often acts as an entry mechanism for new filmmakers who haven't the reputation to secure a major production at a big studio. Producer Neil Moritz preferred first-time director Jonathan Liebesman for the $70 million *Battle: LA*, which earned $212 million worldwide due to its military-extraterrestrial theme. That film earned him entry into a very competitive film industry. Liebesman referred to his aliens as "genocidal Nazis...They look at us like we look at ants." As another example, the Angelina Jolie written-and-directed film, *In the Land of Blood and Honey* (2011), set in the Bosnian War, had a budget of $13 million and earned only $300,000. Compare this also to *The Invasion* (2007)—a troubled $80 million remake of the 1956 *Invasion of the Body Snatchers*—which still pulled in $40 million worldwide despite being reviewed as "soulless" and "uninspired."

It isn't unusual to see the continuation of the evil alien theme through the modern day alongside the continuation of the UFO Cover-Up. There is plenty of material—false and true—to feed storytellers for many more years to come. The absence of the benevolent or altruistic ET race in these expensive science fiction tentpole pictures has everything to do with the surreptitious avoidance to inform the public that earth has been visited and that governments have signed agreements with nonhuman cultures. The idea that a UFO can crash in 1947 and is never followed by any alien invasion whatsoever and yet, at the same time, people can go into a theatre to watch, in detail, exactly how an advanced race would attempt to destroy mankind, is rooted in deception.

Had any of the hundreds of significant UFO sightings over the years been real, it would indicate that the aliens are already on the planet and within our skies, but what's interesting is that there's never been any kind of invasion or mass murder. Unfortunately, there's not much view interest in altruistic extraterrestrial races, not according to science fiction filmmakers who are determined to continue to use the age-old formula. And to present human beings as earth's moral defenders, rather than psychotic and primitive, as when compared to a million-year of this tiny planet. And films that attempt to blow that evolutionary line such as *John Carter* (2012), a disappointing live-action debut Andrew Stanton, are likely to fail and fail big. Although the picture amassed $284 million in four months, the Walt Disney Company issued a financial statement in May that attributed an $84 million loss on John Carter. Subsequently, Rich Ross, the head of Walt Disney Studios, was fired. Soderbergh's meditative psychodrama *Solaris* (2002), a remake based on a sci-fi novel by Polish writer Stanislaw Lem, earned $30 million in box-office against an estimated $47 million budget. Lem himself was disappointed that the filmmakers focused on the psychological theme rather than the vast alien ocean that the astronauts had communicated with.

After a recent period of unsuccessful remakes, *Race to Witch Mountain* (2009), and media franchise extensions, *Transformers 4: Age of Extinction (2014)*, the film industry is leaning toward science fiction reboots such *as Star Wars* and *Star Trek* with entirely new cast members and modernized storylines. *Star Trek Into Darkness* (2013) had a $190 million budget, was directed by J.J. Abrams, it brought in a whopping $470 million. *Star Trek 3* is currently filming in Vancouver, BC for a 2016 release. Interestingly, the screenwriters plan on returning to the roots of the classic *Star Trek TV* series as the first two films turned into a sort of *Star Wars* resume for Abrams. Now that he got the job to direct the seventh installment of *Star Wars, The Force Awakens,* we should be seeing how the Resistance (Rebels) holds up against the First Order (Empire) some 30 years into the future. Lucasfilm was bought by the Walt Disney Company in 2012 and has announced big plans to expand the Star Wars universe in the future. Hasbro and Paramount announced plans in 2015 to expand the *Transformers* "cinematic universe" to leverage the $3.7 billion haul so far from the first four films. They hope to follow the Disney model for *Star Wars*.

As long as there is money to be made, filmmakers will find access to adequate financial funds and military support to continue to bring fresh and innovative extraterrestrial threats to the human race. Anyone who understands the complexity of culture and the common characteristics of any ethnic identity understands that culture is an expression of a cohesive population. Cultural identities form over time and distinctive differences between ethnic groups separate one nation from another nation. It can be said that the monsters, even if human-looking, found in alien cinema all seem to share the same type of culture, and it is a culture that is as arrogant as it is violent, as dedicated to colonial expansion as it is to its galactic goals of dominion.

SPEAKER: Our projections show that by the year 2025, not only America, but the entire planet will be under the protection and the dominion of this power alliance. The gains have been substantial. Both for ourselves and for you, the human power elite!

(wild applause.)

SPEAKER: You have given us entre to the resources we need in our ongoing quest for multidimensional expansion, and in return,

the per capita income each of you tonight has
grown, in this year alone, by an average 39%.

(wild applause.)

They Live (1984)

These galactic ethnic groups, through having
different shapes and sizes and speaking different
languages, all appear to share the same cultural
characteristics, namely they want to compromise
or wipe out the human race. Not only that but
their reasons for doing so are often baseless. And
what's interesting is that the cultural traits of
these psychopathic killers are traceable to their
human counterparts, that is, filmmakers have
not adequately represented an advanced
spacefaring race that is thousands of years ahead
of humanity, rather they have only transposed a
psychopathic faculty of logic onto a nation of
demons.

Audiences, not realizing the involvement of
intelligence agencies in alien cinema, will not
notice the propaganda on the screen. They
haven't created a race of interstellar people, and
this is a central missing point, as they should
have; instead, they've only created new kinds of

imperialists who have better forms of conquering backward civilizations. It also insinuates that extraterrestrial monsters are capitalists, at their core, again another human attribute superimposed over some galactic culture. The insistence that extraterrestrials, comparatively more powerful, are just more corrupt and exploitative versions of humanity are a fundamental flaw of the vast majority of alien-themed science fiction films. It is a flaw because there is no link between capitalism and extraterrestrials. In fact, most offworld cultures are cashless. They don't even wear watches, so how they can they arrive to a business appointment on time?

Film libraries have remained unchanged since the earliest recollections of extraterrestrial contact, and there has not been one ethnic study of *nonhumans* likely a result of incomplete evidence as to their existence in the first place. Screenwriters and producers of alien-themed science fiction films have little or no expertise in their subjects and most often just gleaned the necessary plot details from a UFO documentary to make an interesting story. The monsters of the 1950s and 1960s demonstrated a genuine fear and apprehension of early contact with nonhuman races. Audiences grew more and more accustomed to watching horror stories, looking forward to new kinds of creatures, on the silver screen. The common film formula, "evil alien invasion," likely starting in 1953, was widely used decade after decade as a means to profitability without filmmakers realizing that the formula was also a Pavlovian tool for societal conditioning. Invasion pieces had every kind of space monster and each new filmmaker was to invent an even more diabolical creature.

Is it any wonder that 75% of all alien films over a 65 year period involve an alien invasion?

CHAPTER 5
Independence Day

ALIEN: *Release me... release me...*

US PRESIDENT: You know there's much we can learn from each other if we can negotiate a truce. We can find a way to co-exist. Can there be a peace between us?

ALIEN: *Peace? No peace.*

US PRESIDENT: What is it you want us to do?

ALIEN: *Die... die...*

Independence Day (1996)

Released on July 3, 1996, the alien invasion extravaganza *Independence Day*, directed by Roland Emmerich, brought in $817 million worldwide. The film ran in theatres until January 12, 1997, filling nearly 3,000 theatres. Co-written by Dean Devlin and Emmerich, the disaster flick centered on an interplanetary invasion by an extremely hostile alien race bent on decimating the world on the American Day of

Independence, July 4. It fitted patriotism into alien invasions with unusual skill and panache. Coming off the success of *Stargate* (1994), Emmerich and Devlin, while on a month long vacation in Mexico wrote *Independence Day*. They took it to 20th Century Fox. Twenty-four hours later the project was greenlit. Three days later it went into preproduction and handed a $75 million budget. The director of *The Day After Tomorrow* and *10,000 BC* convinced a discriminatory Hollywood system to accept Will Smith, a black actor, as one of his lead characters.

The advanced aliens and their city-wide motherships invaded the Earth for reasons never explained. When the US President, asks, "What is it you want us to do?" The alien POW says, "Die.... Die!" The only reason for annihilating an entire species is never explained. The invaders apparently have the technological capacity to build motherships, force fields, plasma weapons, and on top of that they live in biomechanical suits and they are all telepathic. Oh yeah, I forgot—they are really ugly.

The movie, dressed in camp and dumb theories is presented as entertainment. As an example, characters fly into outerspace (having never been outside Earth's atmosphere with a starship) to upload a computer virus into the mothership, which defeats the alien software and instantaneously deactivates the defense shields of 100,000 ships. I don't think "absurdity" describes it well enough. *The New York Times* movie reviewer, Caryn James, said, "The film's fun comes from an outrageous scenario that as every review has noted, owes its life to B movies." (July 21, 1996) What most audiences don't understand is that the filmmakers didn't do a shred of research. Neither Devlin nor Emmerich have any understanding of extraterrestrial lore and yet were not only able to write an extraterrestrial story, but also managed to convince 20th Century Fox to give them $75 million. The film studio doesn't appear to scrutinize film properties for authenticity, at least not in this case.

What's interesting in the film is how much UFO lore is tucked into the script. One of the plot points included Area 51 and the capture of an alien spacecraft from Roswell, New Mexico. It so happened that the spacecraft belonged to the alien invaders and wasn't severely damaged, that is, it was in flying condition. *Independence Day* also highlighted the fact that national security always knew about aliens and that the president had been kept out of the loop. The film plays its card very well and slowly builds a military response to the far-advanced alien attack. Most of the film shows Americans under attack. Cities are completely destroyed. America is at a standstill. The aliens are laughing, until finally the president pulls out his megaphone and makes a patriotic speech, "We will not go quietly into the night!" The interplanetary war is on.

The problem with ID4 is that the entire premise is rooted in alien disinformation straight out of the CIA and NSA headquarters. The bigger problem is that this script could never have been written without exclusive access to the disinformation creators. Scene after scene the film peels away the deception, revealing the incredible fear and hatred pervasive in the UFO business: the animosity of all alien life forms, the ugly space monster, the war against aliens as necessity, the secrets in military installations, the fact that aliens have visited before, the back-engineering of technologies, take your pick.

Without any admitted research, or research specifics, it is nearly impossible to write this kind of story in 30 days and then to have it greenlit in 24 hours. This isn't an anomaly. This has the hallmark of a tactic, a tactic centered in psychological operations.

The film contents convince us that aliens are evil and must be destroyed, and they do so in an outrageous way so that we don't see the film for what it is. The film is nothing short of racial discrimination. Had Emmerich dressed up a story about an evil Jewish sect invading New York for their bagels, you can be certain that the entire Jewish community would have outright banned the film. Had Emmerich dressed up a story about evil Chinese invaders who attack America with magic dumplings that can obliterate entire cities, you can be certain that the nation of China would have banned the film.

You might be thinking that my examples are unjust and ridiculous. To me they are as unjust and ridiculous as evil aliens invading Earth in giant spaceships. Emmerich never explains why they're invading. He paints them as space monsters. He turns them into mass murderers and then justifies a war against them. Audiences drink this up. Propaganda wasn't so easily handed out in *The Interview* (2014), starring buddies James Franco and Seth Rogan, a film about two media men who are given the chance to interview the North Korean leader, Kim Jong-Un, and then are hired by the CIA to assassinate him. North Korea said the political satire was an insult and considered it "a most blatant act of terrorism and war" and promised that a "merciless counter-measure" would result. Columbia Pictures delayed the release by three months. Death threats were made to theatres that planned to screen the film. Sony Pictures pulled the film and the associated websites. Hollywood fumbled the ball. Then in November, Sony computers were hacked by pro-North Korean hackers who stole 30,000 corporate documents. It caused a public embarrassment and a reaction across the board because a Communist dictatorship had forced a major US company into self-censorship. President Obama weighed in on the scandal saying, "We cannot have a society in which some dictator some place can start imposing censorship here in the United States." Senator John McCain considered the Sony hack an "act of war." George Clooney said,

"We cannot be told we can't see something by Kim Jong-un, of all fucking people." *The Interview* release was mostly scrapped and released primarily via online download on December 24, 2014. The story didn't end there. On April 16, 2015, six months after the hack, WikiLeaks, an online publisher of newsworthy leaks, posted all 30,287 Sony documents (including emails) online with a searchable database. Sony rebuked the action.

On April 18, 2015 Emmerich announced two additional cast members, Bill Pullman and Judd Hirsch, who will be joining the sequel *Independence Day 2* for wide release on June 24, 2016, its twentieth anniversary. Liam Hemsworth is replacing Smith who declined to reprise his role, which was a smart thing to do considering that the sequel is just another digital load of misinformation. The story is supposedly about a human-led invasion on the alien planet (surprise!). A very important and often neglected fact—people who make alien films can say whatever they want about extraterrestrial races, painting them evil 91% of the time, because there's no backlash or retaliation.

It isn't necessary to study the subject when all you have to study is the toilet. Worse, audience members whose brain mechanisms have been squandered by decades of deceit see nothing wrong with these pseudo-scientific B movies, often equating them to "popcorn entertainment." Films that wholeheartedly discriminate against advanced interstellar cultures are not popcorn entertainment, and that is the crux of the problem—audiences have been brainwashed.

You advance a person into a monk in 25 years. He understands the Universe and God. You advance that monk ahead 1,000 years, what does he do? He builds a starship and finds another galaxy. According to Hollywood, you advance him 10,000 years ahead, he reverts into a genocidal maniac, flies back to the Earth and tries to wipe out the human race. And the reason? No reason. He doesn't need a reason because he understands God and the Universe!

The fact that audiences do not see the woefully negative portrayal of aliens as odd is evidence that they do not see clearly, or don't care. They don't question what they are shown because they are shown so much of the same garbage. That all points back to Pavlov and his loyal dog that salivated every time he rang a bell.

Film audiences, and the general public, may believe in UFOs and the presence of extraterrestrials, what they don't know is that their government *knows* about UFOs and extraterrestrials, and governmental agencies have learned to cooperate with Hollywood studios, for national security reasons I'm sure, and their goal is to make sure you are deathly afraid of anything with an alien origin. The thought implant is so deep now that it is doubtful that anyone over 30 can overcome its effects. And how do you clear your mind of decades of lies? Where do you search for the truth?

CHAPTER 6
Church of the Alien God

Given the antiquated and derogatory nature of anti-alien films it is strange that filmmakers still feel inspired to make this kind of story and to sell it to large-scale audiences. Any genre steeped in deeply negative and uncharacteristic depictions of their subject, even if that subject has been officially stamped by the government, exists in the category of propaganda. And hate propaganda (and hate speech) is generally frowned upon in the modern world. Apparently, alien films are not included. "Aliens aren't real!" They remain largely tolerated by the mainstream public, even watched by people who believe that UFOs are real.

What drives a filmmaker to make a film? What motivates them to pursue a story right through fruition? Filmmaking is a very strange business. The old model of filmmaking would take a surprise cinematic hit like Spielberg's *Jaws* (1975, $470 million), based on the Peter

Benchley novel, and stitch together a sequel *Jaws 2* (1978, $180 million) to cash in on the box office fever. Film producers were interested in making money. That model was revised, later, when audiences complained that the first film was better written, directed and acted, and the sequel paled in comparison. To that end, the original filmmaker was usually not present. Spielberg opted out of *Jaws 2*.

Slowly, urged by the growing taste of audiences, filmmakers began to spend as much time on a sequel as on the original film. It took a very long time for filmmaking to reach a point where producers moved away from the *Weekend at Bernie's 2* (1993) and *Caddyshack 2* (1988) strategy, something filmmakers experience after an overnight success, and began to adopt a business building model. Hence, the slow rise of the alien franchise.

The first science fiction film franchise with an alien theme was *Star Wars*, released in 1977. The sequel, *The Empire Strikes Back* (1980), is still regarded as the best in the franchise. *Return of the Jedi* (1983) followed, still well regarded, and closed off the original trilogy. George Lucas was a maverick filmmaker. After *Star Wars* became a success, bringing in $1.8 billion over its release history, he began to fund his own films, completing another 3 prequels in the anthology, and built a $4 billion empire later bought by Disney. Three more sequels (Episodes VII, VIII, IX) plus other stories in the anthology are all in various stages of production.

Ridley Scott is famous for directing *Blade Runner* (1982), starring Han Solo himself Harrison Ford, a story of android insurgents and based on the work of author Philip K. Dick. Scott was also responsible for launching the *Alien* film franchise in 1979. The original starred a young Sigourney Weaver whose character faced an alien serial killer on board the spaceship *Nostromo*. The Giger-inspired designs for the "alien in a costume" also inspired James Cameron, fresh from the success of his debut *The Terminator* (1984), to make the 1986 sequel *Aliens*. The sequel was a remarkable improvement to the original concept, expanding the universe, all the while keeping the entertainment value high. *Aliens* became a model for other science fiction sequels and *Alien 3* (1992), directed by David Fincher (who later disowned the final cut), brought in $160 million. Five years later, there was *Alien Resurrection*.

Following the release of *Alien 4*, and the two crossover films *Alien vs. Predator* in 2004 and 2007, Scott and Cameron began to revisit the story. Scott eventually directed and produced a prequel, set 30 years before the 1979 story, resulting in *Prometheus* (2012). The film was set in the Zeta 2 Reticuli system at a secret military bioweapons lab run by alien giants. It brought in a global box office of $400 million, not bad for an idea more than 30 years old. *Prometheus*, named after the ship carrying the human crew, mixed old and new elements, sometimes in jarring ways, and Scott later announced the production of *Prometheus 2*, to be released in 2016. The film is reportedly moving away from the original xenomorph designs. The final result is still unknown. In fact, it is nearly impossible to predict how any film will turn out due to the nature of filmmaking. We can imagine that *Prometheus 2* will be a visionary film set in a distant planet with an amazing conclusion about the human race, and with aliens with bad dispositions. I doubt that the "Engineers" have any monks among their species.

We're seeing the continuation of what is invariably an anti-alien idea, for those that are aware of offplanet races on or near the planet, and it is being propagated and funded through a legitimate distribution system. This is because audiences do not understand the underlying agenda at display on the giant movie screen. It may seem that I am against entertainment and anything to interfere with popcorn sales. I love cinema and I love being entertained by cinematic stories. Like I said, I've written for the screen. The perpetuation of a story that denigrates and demoralizes anything "alien," and that is rooted in horror, terror and fear, is a legal way to attack the hearts and minds of society. The global society is being mind-controlled.

I bet you were thinking that the *Alien* franchise was out of ideas. Well, they're not. A little after the release of *Prometheus*, the director of *District 9* started talking to Weaver about the *Alien* films. That talk inspired Neill Blomkamp, who worked with Weaver on the $50 million *Chappie* (2015), to begin developing concept art for an *Alien 5*. Blomkamp, desperate to continue where Scott and Cameron left off, and needing to generate some studio sparks, posted some of his art on Instagram. The effect worked to get Alien 5 greenlit with Weaver and even Michael Biehn (*Aliens*) and Sharlto Copley (*District 9*) on board. Live long the xenomorph that eats people because it is always hungry!

What is driving this incessant need to demoralize and discredit alien life forms? Think of it another way, do you think any of the multiple and intelligent writers for these films has ever done a proper investigation of extraterrestrial cultures? Have they ever attended a UFO conference? Have they interview people who have been contacted by star visitors? The evidence is clearly on screen. There is no understanding of interstellar culture. Even 30 years later, Scott tries to remove himself from the alien xenomorph and in its place he adds the *Engineers*, an extraterrestrial race of giants who have perfected planetary genocide. *Prometheus* contained a plot device to destroy Earth using biological weapons. Here again we meet the repeated theme of *Alien* movies: First there was the serial killer on a ship (*Alien*), then there was an alien infestation on a planetoid (*Aliens*), some more serial killing (*Alien 3*) and as the story progress (*Alien 4*) we were only to discover that the original xenomorphs were part of a plan to commit interplanetary genocide (*Prometheus*).

What is feeding this need to make these films? *Prometheus* cost $130 million to make. Add marketing and promotion it could very well reach $180 million (in Hollywood terms). One hundred and eighty million dollars to make a horror movie? The model for making horror movies is to keep the budget low. *Paranormal Activity*, about a haunted family, was made for $15,000. Bought by Paramount and released wide, the film earned $200 million at the box office. *Jaws* was made for $9 million and earned $470 million. That is the model for making money with a movie. Scary movies tend to be low budget and tend to make money, and if they don't then producers don't lose their shirts.

The entire alien film genre is rooted in horror and terror. Some of these films have been remade since the original film was released—*The Thing, Invasion of the Body Snatchers, War of the Worlds, The Day the Earth Stood Still, The Blob.* Many of these films have sequels: *Predator, Men in Black, Species, Transformers,*

Independence Day. Has there ever been a sequel to *Close Encounters of the Third Kind* or *Starman*? No. Why? No one wants to do any research!

In the Cameron-directed big-budget *The Abyss* (1989), starring Ed Harris and Biehn, the centrepiece of the story included an advanced underwater alien species that had not only mastered control of water molecules, more importantly, the race was altruistic. They lived at the bottom of the ocean and never planned an evil alien invasion.

Is what perpetuates alien horror films ignorance? Are filmmakers and screenwriters simply too ignorant to know the difference? Or is it that filmmakers want to make money and evil aliens simply pull more in at the box office. Is this need to discredit advanced people based solely on money? That might a good reason, but it doesn't explain why anyone would invest $180 million to make *Prometheus*. Not if you wanted to make money. The model to make money is to spend as little as possible and to maximize profits. The only people who would toss $180 million into a project are those building a church.

Filmmakers don't build churches. Or do they? A church is built because of belief and faith. It's not built to make money. Churches are built to spread the holy word. Churches are made to save people and to expand the flock. If filmmakers aren't building churches but they're over-spending on poorly researched and discriminatory films, the only logical conclusion would be to feed an agenda. To feed a fever.

I wonder if it's possible that alien films are spurred on by some kind of "interstellar virus." That truly would be an effective way for aliens to invade the Earth, wouldn't it? An interstellar virus could be the driving force behind the continued discrimination of false alien beliefs, and since there's no interstellar liaison office to protect the image of nonhumans then filmmakers can basically do whatever they can get away with. That is, as long as audiences put up with it.

Audiences shouldn't put up with it if they want to see an eventual reconciliation between humans and nonhumans. A negative climate and an embedded derogatory image of interstellar races are very effective ways in which intelligence and military operatives destabilize the enemy. By adjusting the perception of an alien and coloring that perception in fear, the propagandists have ensured the postponement of any meaningful contact.

When you measure the global box office push of anti-alien propaganda, since it cannot simply be described as solely entertainment anymore, you get a sense as to the will and determination involved. The alien genre generated $6 billion globally. Imagine I gave you $6 billion to discredit, deceive and demoralize the presence of interstellar cultures on Earth. If you do it openly, that is, if people were aware of extraterrestrials, then your films would all be considered against nonhumans. And there are laws against discrimination. There's no law against alien discrimination if aliens don't officially exist.

I think it would make sense for audience members to look at every alien film and to ask if the filmmakers did any research. Ask them specifically what research they did and how their research always comes up with grotesque space monsters.

Audiences would discover that zero research was done and it all came from the imagination of the filmmakers and funded by the clandestine budget of the producers. Verily, we know that the CIA and the Pentagon are embedded in the filmmaking business, and we know these organizations have large and mysterious bank accounts. I like to think of big budget alien films as made by these organizations because I cannot fathom a film producer interested in building churches, and I can see the CIA building churches.

CHAPTER 7
The Evolution of the Alien

In 1951, the alien was depicted as a human-looking interplanetary ambassador buoyed by an assortment of ultra-advanced technological tools, including a fully-functional robot and a gleaming starship. That was the portrait of an alien in *The Day the Earth Stood Still*. By 1986, the alien had become a hoard of xenomorphs and a foreign threat that needed to be wiped out. In *Aliens*, Ripley joins a team of over-confident space marines who descend on LV-426 with all the jingoism from the Vietnam War. It only took 35 years to brainwash the world to hate extraterrestrials.

Ten years later, *Independence Day* hit theatres and solidified our deep fear of space. Filmmakers were reinforcing the fact that whatever was in outer space was to be feared. The original slogan from *Alien* was hard and fast: "In space no one can hear you scream." We started with an interstellar savior in the fifties.

The sixties were all about the alleged moon landing. The seventies warmed up with *Star Wars* and ended with the fear of space. The eighties became about the militarization of space. The nineties was when the entire space tried to annihilate humankind. By 2005, Spielberg joined Tom Cruise in a $130 million remake of *War of the Worlds*. Giant alien war machines burst through the crust to wipe us out. Two years later, Spielberg's protégé Michael Bay directs the $150 million *Transformers*, about giant alien war machines that can dance, talk and destroy cities. Where did we start? We started with a man and his starship. Where are we now? Utter chaos.

   If a genuine traveler from outer space were to land today the first thing that would happen is that people would run off screaming. The tanks would roll in. B-2 stealth bombers would be given new headings and a hoard of drones would be deployed to estimate the size of the threat. You may think that I am exaggerating. You might even think that I do not understand human behavior. I am not like most people in the sense that I do not underestimate the will of mankind's masters. Because until now I have yet to see any real activism against the mass of anti-alien propaganda. The situation is so severe that the term "anti-alien propaganda" was only recently invented, by me.

I invented the term "anti-alien propaganda" and that is because no one understood that they were watching discriminatory and derogatory films against all interstellar and interdimensional cultures. Since aliens in general, even the altruistic ones, do not have an active system of rebuttal, or have a higher tolerance for childish antics from the clandestine agencies, they are at the mercy of the audience and the movie critics. These people, unfortunately, have never been properly educated in extraterrestrial lore because their governments have classified all materials on ET contact.

In summary, the false characteristics of extraterrestrial life forms—serial killers, mass murderers, genocidal maniacs, warmongers, homicidal maniacs, megalomaniacs, egomaniacs, and eugenicists—have all been concocted and established since the 1950s, several years after the Roswell crash in New Mexico and the establishment of the National

Security Act in the United States. Filmmakers are interested in maximizing the profits and exposure of any of their film properties. Alien franchises, because they tend to have an established (cult) following, have become better instruments at making money. As long as the sequel is an improvement over the earlier version, audiences will continue coming back, and if the film sucks the entire world will hear about it online. Movies depicting altruistic aliens don't earn as much money at the box office and cater to a smaller crowd. The conditions of the market will dictate what kind of film best satisfies the largest audience demand. Like we saw through the decades, the alien has gone through a perpetual state of metamorphosis that has no bearing whatsoever with reality. It is a movie creature and movie creatures get copyrights.

There was a remarkable shift in the summer of 2014 after the release of Marvel's *Guardians of the Galaxy*, starring Chris Pratt and Zoe Saldana. The James Gunn-directed $200 million film went onto a surprise box office success and Pratt's congenial "Star-Lord" entered our vocabulary. *Guardians* earned a 91% approval rating on *Rotten Tomatoes*, a movie review aggregator. Hefty budget, intergalactic travel, planetary wars—only this film lacked the standardized alien nut because in the cosmos everyone is alien. In fact, of the 5 superheroes only one was human (Peter Quill). The other four were made up of a walking tree (Groot), a mutated wise-cracking raccoon (Rocket), a female assassin with green skin (Gamora) and an alien warrior with red skin (Drax). And that's the biggest surprise after all these years of anti-alien filmmaking. Here was a film starring aliens, even ugly aliens, and they were out to protect the galaxy from destruction. Audiences helped the film earn $775 million.

My book isn't about the challenges of making films, so I don't feel it my duty having to justify why any one film turned out the way it did. Producing films is a difficult business and I don't want to come across as a film critic. My interests are about the depiction of nonhuman life forms on the cinematic and television screen, or digital download, and how their depiction is largely unbalanced, misguided and racially-biased. There are movies I have not seen and there are films that if examined closely reveal a much richer characterisation than I may have noticed. I have focused on the larger trends (more than 250 films) in the movie industry that has shaped the way we perceive spacefaring cultures. A film producer may only be focused on getting a film property greenlit because their paycheck is dependent upon production, and may not find any financial compensation in properly researching the extraterrestrial subject. The mass of careless alien characterizations in the market only supports my argument. I have the evidence. Furthermore, film producers also come out of intelligence agencies (eg CIA) and they generally have access to a good amount of financing and silent partners. Film production studios also hire low level agents, even if unknowingly, who start off in script reading, filtering out any material that may be deemed unfit for the Pavlovian market. A CIA co-produced film does not come with a CIA press kit. Agents work undercover. Assets work in conjunction with agents and everyone is connected to a wide network of media agencies that are all competent in the dissemination of ideas.

I have not explained the exact nature of an interstellar culture as this is outside the parameters of this book. They are no different than any other intelligent life forms. Each race carries a set of cultural values and shared knowledge. Advanced races of beings tend to have escaped the confines of egotism. They have surpassed the need to believe in God. They understand DNA. Some have struggled with their ego knowing that it is a struggle they must win. Does that make those few genocidal maniacs? I think it takes a lot of work to become a lunatic. What is true is that alien races tend to think on a different track and make multidimensional decisions, and these decisions can be misunderstood by those whose mind can only perceive three dimensions. What is also true is that there are organizations on Earth that are funded to deceive people and to discredit any genuine contact attempts by the altruistic races. They will twist my words. Even if someone was to meet a couple of aliens that same person would be followed up with a series of attacks that would destroy any future cooperation. Likewise, a screenwriter intending to write a fair script involving aliens may also find themselves inclined to follow the usual course or to be blacklisted. Sometimes it is because the liaison for the Pentagon has made a few suggestions before handing over the aircraft carrier keys and sometimes there are strange dreams of evil monsters that would be cooler if they were to be put on screen.

What all this says is that it takes a lot of determination to present the facts and to have those facts represented on screen as originally intended. Is that even possible in the movie industry? Whenever you watch a movie you are seeing the fine art of compromise. The other issue is the brainwashed market who demands scary aliens in space simply because that's the only thing they seem to understand, and producers cannot justify a film containing altruistic aliens because that is not what the market demands. The idea that filmmakers want to make money is one of those fuzzy ideas in the art business. Film is art. The 1963 Andy Warhol painting *Silver Car Crash (Double Disaster)* sold for $105 million in November 2013. Art is irrational.

Film is church. Filmmakers make films they believe in. They make films they've had in their minds for 20 years. They make films they love. Studios don't dish out $200 million to make a movie because they want to make money because if they wanted to make money they'd make 10 movies with a budget of $20 million each. I am not one to buy the film business argument all the time, especially since I know that many films are propagandist tools disguised as entertainment.

An educated moviegoer should be able to walk into a movie theatre and to realize right away if this movie tells a story or if this movie has a story to tell. When it comes to alien-themed movies, we have to be aware that these entertainment pieces are coated with disinformation and deception even though they are dressed in fun and special effects. Actors should be aware that they are being used to further an agenda. Celebrities should demand a more rigorous reworking of the main characters in a screenplay about aliens.

The reason why there is so much propaganda is because there is plan on the table to keep humans separate from nonhumans. That plan has been in effect for a very long time and the agencies involved will do whatever it takes to keep society glued onto all the wrong things. We now know that the evil space monster is the wrong thing to be looking at and anyone perpetuating this idea is probably infected with that interstellar virus that is going around Hollywood.

The alien hasn't evolved since 1951.

EPILOGUE
The End of the Extraterrestrial

Alien cinema is still a relatively new cinema having only been formed since 1950, but it is also a way being used to document an aspect of society that has been vehemently suppressed. It could almost be said that all alien-themed science fiction films, because they are based on real facts and actual discriminatory tactics and biased views, are documentaries disguised as entertainment. A UFO documentary can never compete, and has never competed, at the box office with a *District 9* (2009), $210 million in worldwide revenue, or *Men in Black 3* (2012), earning $600 million worldwide.

Central to the interstellar narrative are government agents and unclassified military agencies that are paid to interfere with all extraterrestrial activity. Aliens in films are perceived as threats that need to be eliminated at whatever cost. In my analysis of 250 alien-themed films (see Appendix for the complete list) the alien invasion formula is present in three out of every four movies. Here we can say that there is a 75% chance that the first mothership to grace our skies will do so only to invade the planet. Indeed, the significance of this fact suggests that there is nothing offplanet that would be beneficial to humanity. To even think of outer space is to instantly be repulsed by it.

Frankly, alien cinema has been hijacked by both intelligence and military interests, having thrown out any cultural values that advanced races carry, in order to ensure that society does not befriend any nonhuman cultures because all of that would undermine 65 years of propaganda, deception, and defamation against actual extraterrestrials. This goes against the facts of history which contain evidence of interstellar visitations, cultural exchanges, historical artifacts, and even signs of genetic manipulation. Audiences have allowed these distortions to take place because each new generation has entered society further and further from the truth.

Canadian Human Rights Act
3. (1) For all purposes of this Act, the
prohibited grounds of discrimination are
race, national or ethnic origin, colour,
religion, age, sex, sexual orientation,
marital status, family status, disability
and conviction for an offense for which a
pardon has been granted or in respect of
which a record suspension has been
ordered.

With 90% of alien cinema portraying evil alien
monsters engulfed in expensive military theatres
of engagement, it is clear that the disinformation
agents hold the dominant position over UFO
secrets, both domestically and internationally.
The presence of dominance, in regards to
cultural exchange and cooperation has led to a
perennial clash of civilizations and the
prevention of any belated UFO disclosure. All of
this has been artificially constructed in an
ongoing attempt to marginalize and trivialize
one of the most important topics on the planet.
What we are seeing in movie theatres is the kind
of hate propaganda and racial discrimination
that would never be accepted in front of any
human rights tribunal and neither should

audiences accept these discriminatory practices as blockbuster entertainment.

The filmmakers of alien cinema, because of their cartoonish depiction of advanced cosmic beings and their unwillingness to educate themselves and to expand the genre in meaningful ways, are projecting their own fears and childhood fantasies onto the screen in order to terrorize audiences who after decades of brainwashing are no better educated than the filmmakers. If you were to go into an insane asylum and handed each patient a packet of crayons and a sketch book you would invariably get the monstrosities commonly found in alien-themed films, at a much cheaper price than is currently being paid.

This shared relationship between the storyteller and the extraterrestrial audience becomes a platform for acute intelligence disinformation transfer and saves clandestine agencies from ever admitting what they already know about star visitors. It is also a cost-effective way to control and distort highly-classified and unclassified information. By way of media entertainment, agencies such as the CIA and the NSA can misinform millions of people and to compartmentalize details on extraterrestrial activity on the planet, and to do so while earning a profit and each new idea given a $100 million marketing push.

People are paying to be deceived, all the while satisfying their interstellar curiosity and once that curiosity has been satiated, regardless if the information is correct or not, they no longer have any questions. This perpetual system of brainwashing has preternaturally delayed any necessary UFO disclosure or interstellar reconciliation. We should enhance our understanding of interstellar cultures and strengthen the bonds between planetary and interplanetary groups, rather than to rely on the status quo.

There are many ways that a film reaches the cinema. I have not said that filmmaking is easy and that individual filmmakers are purposely discriminating against all alien races. There's no way for me to know the backstories of each and every production. I cannot identify all the undercover agents or the intelligence assets. It is sometimes hard to distinguish between patriotism and wrongful intention. A person with an agenda doesn't usually inform others of the agenda unless they all belong to the same society. Logic is one way for me to disassociate general ignorance with collusion. Spending $150 million to make an alien invasion film remake, as far as I'm concerned, is a way to further an agenda and is a tactic used widely in mind control to reinforce the status quo. The agencies that started the evil space monster trend set the status quo and if you stray from the status quo you will not make money. So what does a filmmaker do? They keep their head inside the status quo without ever realizing the origin of the status quo, an origin that is deeply connected to the National Security Act of 1947, established in the very same month as the saucer crash at Roswell, New Mexico.

The process of turning extraterrestrial stories into global entertainment franchises is long and complicated. It can rarely be pinpointed on any individual person. Filmmaking is a people business consisting of shared ideas. Film genres become problematic when those shared ideas are selling the exact agenda of homeland security. You can see how the patriotism fits in. American storytelling is centered on American culture and if America is under any threat, even if it has tentacles and arrives in a giant mothership, then that threat must be eliminated. The standard xenophobic response is almost expected among loyalists. With a little insight and wisdom we can see that the alien races cruising through outer space and in other dimensions have not all heard of the planet Earth. Even having heard of it, their immediate reaction would not include a full-scale invasion. What I'm saying is that we are not the only planet in the universe with water, a worn plot device used to justify many alien invasions. If history is correct, the last 12,000 years demonstrates the absence of an alien invasion and the fact that it represents 75% of all alien movies is a testament that the "alien invasion" is just another Hollywood illusion.

APPENDIX

Hollywood Alien Cinema List (by decade)
North American Market

The following list is based on my own personal research. Small films with limited distribution or with unsubstantial alien elements not included. An alien film is any film that contains a significant alien element, theme, or even trigger. A propaganda-free alien film is described as a film that is objectively written and generally unbiased and/or has a very low amount of propaganda or even when the bad propaganda is balanced out with the good propaganda. Some films were marketed under multiple names.

Breakdown

Total Films Overall, 1950-2012: **10,000** (approx.)
Total Alien Films, 1950-2012: **250** (2.5%)
Total Evil Alien Films, 1950-2012: **228** (91%)
Total Propaganda-free Alien Films, 1950-2012: **22** (9%)

Average alien films/year: 4

Total Alien Films (1950-1959): 30
Total Alien Films (1960-1969): 16
Total Alien Films (1970-1979): 27
Total Alien Films (1980-1989): 57
Total Alien Films (1990-1999): 53
Total Alien Films (2000-2009): 49
Total Alien Films (2010): 2
Total Alien Films (2011): 10
Total Alien Films (2012): 6

1950s

1. Rocketship X-M (1950)
2. Flight to Mars (1950)
3. Destination Moon (1950)
4. The Man from Planet X (1950)
5. The Thing from Another World (1951)
6. The Day the Earth Stood Still (1951)
7. Robot Monster (1953)
8. Invaders from Mars (1953)
9. Abbott and Costello Go to Mars (1953)
10. It Came From Outer Space (1953)
11. The War of the Worlds (1953)
12. Devil Girl from Mars (1953)
13. The Creature from the Black Lagoon (1954)
14. This Island Earth (1955)
15. Forbidden Planet (1956)
16. Earth vs. The Flying Saucers (1956)
17. Invasion of the Body Snatchers (1956)
18. Invasion of the Saucer-Men (1957)

19. 20 Million Miles to Earth (1957)

20. Not of this Earth (1957)

21. The Mysterians (1957)

22. Destroy All Monsters (1957)

23. The Blob (1958)

24. It! The Terror from Beyond Space (1958)

25. I Married a Monster from Outer Space (1958)

26. The Trollenberg Terror (1958)

27. Plan 9 from Outer Space (1959)

28. Teenagers from Outer Space (1959)

29. The Angry Red Planet (1959)

30. Battle in Outer Space (1959)

1960s

31. The Cape Canaveral Monsters (1960)

32. First Men in the Moon (1964)

33. Wizard of Mars (1964)

34. Dr. Who and the Daleks (1965)

35. The Human Duplicators (1965)(various titles)

36. The Wizard of Mars (1965)(various titles)

37. Dalek's Invasion Earth: 2150 A.D. (1966)

38. Dr. Terror's Gallery of Horrors (1966)

39. The Time Travellers (1966)

40. Bomb Voyage (1967)

41. They Came from Beyond Space (1967)

42. Quatermass and the Pit (1967)

43. The Incredible Invasion (1968)(various titles)

44. The Monitors (1969)

45. Thin Air (1969)(various titles)

46 Zeta One (1969)(Alien One)

1970S

47. The Andromeda Strain (1971)
48. Beware! The Blob (1972)
49. Solaris (1972)
50. Fantastic Planet (1973)
51. Dark Star (1974)
52. Invasion from Inner Earth (1974)
53. Space is the Place (1974)(various titles)
54. Escape to Witch Mountain (1975)
55. The Giant Spider Invasion (1975)
56. The Giant Space Voyage (1975)
57. Hu-Man 91975)
58. The Man Who Fell to Earth (1976)
59. Alien Prey (1977)
60. Close Encounters of the Third Kind (1977)
61. Cosmos: War of the Planets (1977)
62. Star Wars (1977)
63. Starship Invasions (1977)
64. The War in Space (1977)
65. The Alien Factor (1978)
66. Invasion of the Body Snatchers (1978)
67. Message from Space (1978)
68. Alien (1979)
69. The Alien Encounters (1979)
70. The Black Hole (1979)
71. Moonraker (1979)
72. Star Trek: The Motion Picture (1979)
73. Starcrash

1980s

74. Alien Contamination (1980)

75. Alien Dead (1980)

76. Battle Beyond the Stars (1980)

77. The Empire Strikes Back (1980)

78. Flash Gordon (1980)

79. Hangar 18 (1980)

80. Saturn 3 (1980)

81. Earthbound (1981)

82. Galaxy of Terror (1981)

83. Visitors from the Galaxy (1981)

84. The War of the Worlds: Next Century (1981)

85. Android (1982)

86. Blade Runner (1982)

87. E.T.: the Extra-Terrestrial (1982)

88. Star Trek II: The Wrath of Khan (1982)

89. The Thing (1982)

90. Time Walker (1982)

91. The Atlantis Interceptors (1983)

92. Return of the Jedi (1983)

93. Space Raiders (1983)

94. Spacehunter: Adventures in the Forbidden Zone (1983)

95. Strange Invaders (1983)

96. Wavelength (1983)

97. 2010 (1984)

98. The Adventures of Buckaroo Banzai Across the 8th Dimension (1984)

99. The Brother from Another Planet (1984)

100. Star Trek III: The Search for Spock (1984)

101. The Aurora Encounter (1984)

102. Starman (1984)

103. Cocoon (1985)
104. Enemy Mine (1985)
105. Lifeforce (1985)
106. Morons from Outer Space (1985)
107. Aliens (1986)
108. Critters (1986)
109. Invaders from Mars (1986)
110. Star Crystal (1986)
111. Star Trek IV: The Voyage Home (1986)
112. *batteries not included (1987)
113. Innerspace (1987)
114. Predator (1987)
115. Spaceballs (1987)
116. Alien from LA (1988)
117. Alien Nation (1988)
118. The Blob (1988)(remake)
119. Critters 2: The Main Course (1988)
120. Earth Girls are Easy (1988)
121. Killer Clowns from Outer Space (1988)
122. Mac and Me (1988)
123. My Stepmother is an Alien (1988)
124. Not of this Earth (1988)
125. They Live (1988)
126. The Abyss (1989)
127. Communion (1989)
128. Moontrap (1989)
129. Star Trek V: The Final Frontier (1989)

1990s

130. Fatal Sky (1990)
131. I Come in Peace (1990)
132. Martians Go Home (1990)

133. Metamorphoses: The Alien Factor (1990)
134. Moon 44 (1990)
135. Peacemaker (1990)
136. Predator 2 (1990)
137. Spaced Invaders (1990)
138. Total Recall (1990)
139. Watchers II (1990)
140. Abraxas, Guardians of the Universe (1991)
141. Star Trek VI: The Undiscovered Country (1991)
142. Vegas in Space (1991)
143. Alien 3 (1992)
144. Alien Intruder (1993)
145. Body Snatchers (1993)
146. Fire in the Sky (1993)
147. Oblivion (1994)
148. Stargate (1994)
149. Star Trek Generations (1994)
150. Epsilon (1995)
151. Screamers (1995)
152. Species (1995)
153. 12 Monkeys (1995)
154. Village of the Damned (1995)
155. The Arrival (1996)
157. Crossworlds (1996)
158. Independence Day (1996)
159. Mars Attacks! (1996)
160. Space Truckers (1996)
161. Star Trek: First Contact (1996)
162. Alien Resurrection (1997)
163. Contact (1997)
164. Event Horizon (1997)
165. The Fifth Element (1997)
166. Men in Black (1997)
167. Spaceman (1997)

168. Dark City (1998)
169. The Faculty (1998)
170. Lost in Space (1998)
171. Species II (1998)
172. Sphere (1998)
173. Star Trek: Insurrection (1998)
174. The X-Files (1998)
175. The Astronaut's Wife (1999)
176. Escape from Mars (1999)
177. eXistenZ (1999)
178. Galaxy Quest (1999)
179. The Matrix (1999)
180. My Favourite Martian (1999)
181. Progeny (1999)
182. Star Wars: Episode I: The Phantom Menace (1999)
183. Wing Commander (1999)

2000s

184. Battlefield Earth (2000)
185. Mission to Mars (2000)
186. Pitch Black (2000)
187. Red Planet (2000)
188. What Planet are You From? (2000)
189. Donnie Darko (2001)
190. Ghosts of Mars (2001)
191. K-PAX (2001)
192. Planet of the Apes (2001)(remake)
193. The Adventures of Pluto Nash (2002)
194. Imposter (2002)
195. Men in Black II (2002)
196. Signs (2002)
197. Solaris (2002)
198. Star Trek Nemesis (2002)

199. Star Wars Episode II: Attack of the Clones (2002)
200. Alien Hunter (2003)
201. The Matrix Reloaded (2003)
202. The Matrix Revolutions (2003)
203. Alien vs. Predator (2004)
204. The Chronicles of Riddick (2004)
205. Decoys (2004)
206. The Forgotten (2004)
207. Phil the Alien (2004)
208. Alien Abduction (2005)
209. Doom (2005)
210. Evil Aliens (2005)
211. The Hitchhiker's Guide to the Galaxy (2005)
212. The Island (2005)
213. Star Wars Episode III: Revenge of the Sith (2005)
214. War of the Worlds (2005)
215. Alien vs. Predator: Requiem (2007)
216. The Invasion (2007)
217. The Last Mimzy (2007)
218. Transformers (2007)
219. Alien Raiders (2008)
220. The Day the Earth Stood Still (2008)
221. Meet Dave (2008)
222. Outlander (2008)
223. The X-Files: I Want to Believe (2008)
224. Indiana Jones and the Kingdom of the Crystal Skull (2008)
225. Hancock (2008)
226. Avatar (2009)
227. The Box (2009)
228. District 9 (2009)
229. Knowing (2009)
230. Race to Witch Mountain (2009)
231. Star Trek (2009)

232. Transformers: Revenge of the Fallen (2009)

2010s

233. Predators (2010)
234. Skyline (2010)
235. The Adjustment Bureau (2011)
236. Apollo 18 (2011)
237. Battle: LA (2011)
238. Cowboys & Aliens (2011)
239. The Darkest Hour (2011)
240. I Am Number Four (2011)
241. Paul (2011)
242. Super 8 (2011)
243. The Thing (2011)
244. Transformers: Dark of the Moon (2011)
245. The Avengers (2012)
246. Battleship (2012)
247. John Carter (2012)
248. Men in Black 3 (2012)
249. Prometheus (2012)
250. Total Recall (2012)